GREAT MINDS® WIT & WISDOM

Grade 8 Module 3:
What Is Love?

Student Edition

COPYRIGHT STATEMENT

Table of Contents

Name _____

Date _____ Class _____

Handout 3A: Drama Analysis

Directions: Define the quotes in the chart in your own words using text features and context clues, and then explain what each one reveals about these characters' relationship.

Quote	Meaning	What does this reveal about Lysander and Hermia's relationship?
"Belike for want of rain, which I could well / beteem them from the tempest of my eyes." (1.1.132–133)		
"Then let us teach our trial patience / Because it is a customary cross, / As due to love as thoughts and dreams and sighs," (1.1.154–156)		
"If thou lovest me, then / Steal forth thy father's house tomorrow night" (1.1.165–166)		

Name _____

Date _____   Class _____

Handout 3B: Exemplar Argument Essay

Directions: Over the course of this module, you will work with this essay as an exemplar of argumentative writing. In this lesson, read the title and first paragraph and then highlight the claim.

Is *Pyramus and Thisbe* a Tragedy or a Comedy?

Theseus, the duke in *A Midsummer Night's Dream*, has an important decision to make during his wedding celebration: what to watch. Of all the entertainment available for the evening, he picks the play *Pyramus and Thisbe* because it is advertised as "tragical mirth" (5.1.61). The idea that a play could be both sad and funny, tragic and comic, is intriguing to the duke because they are contradictory ideas, and he calls the idea of a funny tragedy "hot ice" and "wondrous strange snow" (5.1.63). What Theseus, and the audience, learns is that the play, while comically delivered, is truly a tragedy. *Pyramus and Thisbe* is a tragedy because in the action of the play, two young lovers are overwhelmed by outside pressures and commit suicide.

The first point that demonstrates *Pyramus and Thisbe* is a tragedy is that there are outside forces acting on the lovers. From the moment Pyramus appears onstage, it is clear that he faces opposition with regard to his relationship with his lover, Thisbe. Played by Snout the tinker, the wall separates the two lovers, who must whisper "through Wall's chink" (5.1.141), or a small hole, to communicate. This kind of barrier between people in love can make it tough to develop a relationship; the couple cannot even kiss! As Thisbe says, "I kiss the wall's hole, not your lips at all" (5.1.214). The wall separates the lovers, and in that way it is just an obstacle, but it actually represents the reason for the lovers' separation, as Pyramus explains as he waits for Thisbe to appear: "And thou, O wall, O sweet, O lovely wall, / That stand'st between her father's ground and / mine," (5.1.183–185). Therefore, the real division between the two lovers is who owns the wall, Thisbe's father, and the fact that Pyramus cannot get past the wall to Thisbe's family's property. It is true that the play does not reveal any further details about the conflict between Thisbe's father and Pyramus, but it seems unlikely that Pyramus got along with Thisbe's father, since he was whispering to Thisbe through a hole in the wall. Furthermore, if Thisbe's father approved of the lovers' relationship, why would they have to meet face to face in secret? Pressure from outside forces, like a family member from an older generation, is one of the most common reasons for conflict in Shakespearean tragedies. For instance, *Romeo and Juliet* is the most famous example of two lovers who cannot wed because of their families. On a smaller scale, Pyramus and Thisbe experience these same pressures, and this separation and need for secrecy are what cause the couple to meet at "Ninus' tomb" (5.1.147) where they meet their end.

The second point that supports the conclusion that *Pyramus and Thisbe* is a tragedy is the ending of the play. Pyramus and Thisbe are two lovers whose ending is swift, tragic, and permanent. Their plan to meet away from anyone who would object to their union results in each taking his or her own life. Pyramus arrives immediately after Thisbe and finds a bloody piece of clothing. Pyramus exclaims, "lion vile hath here deflowered my dear" (5.1.307) as he mistakenly thinks Thisbe has been killed by an animal. It is then that the play takes a dramatic turn toward tragedy: Pyramus takes out his sword and kills himself, telling the audience "Now am I dead" (5.1.317). Thisbe returns to find her lover's dead body and chooses also to die by the sword (5.1.360–361). The play ends in death, a common trait among tragedies. This tragic ending of the play, a conclusion of death, is important because eliminates any perception that *Pyramus and Thisbe* is a comedy.

Name _____

Date _____ Class _____

There are those who would argue that *Pyramus and Thisbe* is not a tragedy but actually a comedy. The rehearsal and performance of the play are certainly humorous, and the players advertise the play as a comedy, yet this humor has to do with the inexperience and skill of the actors involved and not with the play's content. Within *A Midsummer Night's Dream*, the play is acted by a group of "[h]ard-handed men that work in Athens" (5.1.76) who have never acted before. Their lack of training makes the way the play is performed funny. For instance, when the lion enters onstage, he explains to the audience he is not actually a lion, "Then know that I, as Snug the joiner, am / A lion fell, nor else no lion's dam" (5.1.237–238). This is funny because the audience is supposed to believe he is a lion, and he breaks character to explain to the audience. Another example of this humor is when Bottom, playing Pyramus, mistakes his lines. He tells Thisbe to meet him at "Ninny's tomb" (V.i.215) instead of Ninus' tomb, a mistake that is funny because a ninny is a foolish or silly person. Bottom also refers to the play as a comedy when he says, "There are things in this comedy of Pyramus / and Thisbe that will never please" (3.1.9–10). However, the mistakes of the actors and their (mis)understanding of the play do not change what happens in the play itself. In a Shakespearean comedy, there is a positive end to the conflict. Characters often get married or there is a plan for marriage. The characters certainly do not die at the end. Instead, as in the case of *A Midsummer Night's Dream*, the lovers overcome their obstacles and get married. The performance of *Pyramus and Thisbe* may be extremely silly and poorly acted, but this does not make the play a comedy.

In conclusion, the play of *Pyramus and Thisbe* is a struggle for love that does not end well. Both lovers must keep their relationship a secret from Thisbe's father, and the result of this oppression leads to their deaths, common features of a Shakespearean tragedy. Theseus is pleased with his choice, understanding the tragedy of the play and stating it was "notably discharged" (5.1.377–378), meaning the actors performed their tragedy to the best of their ability. As the duke well knows, there is nothing funny about two people dying for love, and *Pyramus and Thisbe* is no exception.

Name _____

Date _____ Class _____

Handout 4A: Figurative Language Analysis

Directions: Identify three pieces of figurative language from Act 1, Scene 1, lines 183–257 and explain the literal and figurative meanings.

Figurative Language Use the citation style: (Act. Scene. Line(s))	Literal Meaning What is the exact translation of this figurative language?	Figurative Meaning What does this language mean in the context of the play?

Name

_____

Date   Class

_____

Handout 4B: Fluency Homework

Directions:

1. Day 1: Read the text carefully and annotate to help you read fluently.

2. Each day:

    a. Practice reading the text aloud three to five times.

    b. Evaluate your progress by placing a checkmark in the appropriate, unshaded box.

    c. Ask someone (adult or peer) to listen and evaluate you as well.

3. Last day: Answer the self-reflection questions at the end.

HELENA

How happy some o'er other some can be!

Through Athens I am thought as fair as she.

But what of that? Demetrius thinks not so.

He will not know what all but he do know.

And, as he errs, doting on Hermia's eyes,

So I, admiring of his qualities.

Things base and vile, holding no quantity,

Love can transpose to form and dignity.

Love looks not with the eyes but with the mind;

And therefore is winged Cupid painted blind.

Nor hath Love's mind of any judgment taste.

Wings, and no eyes, figure unheedy haste.

And therefore is Love said to be a child

Because in choice he is so oft beguiled.

As waggish boys in game themselves forswear,

So the boy Love is perjured everywhere.

For, ere Demetrius looked on Hermia's eyne,

He hailed down oaths that he was only mine;

And when this hail some heat from Hermia felt,

So he dissolved, and show'rs of oaths did melt.

I will go tell him of fair Hermia's flight.

Then to the wood will he tomorrow night

Pursue her. And, for this intelligence

If I have thanks, it is a dear expense.

But herein mean I to enrich my pain,

To have his sight thither and back again

Shakespeare, William. *A Midsummer Night's Dream*. 1600. Edited by Barbara A. Mowat and Paul Werstine, Simon & Schuster, 2009, 1.1.232–257.

Name _____

Date _____ Class _____

Student Performance Checklist:	Day 1		Day 2		Day 3		Day 4	
	You	Listener*	You	Listener*	You	Listener*	You	Listener*
Accurately read the passage three to five times.								
Read with appropriate phrasing and pausing.								
Read with appropriate expression.								
Read articulately at a good pace and an audible volume.								

*Adult or peer

Self-reflection: What choices did you make about tone and appropriate expression when deciding how to read this passage, and why? What would you like to improve upon or try differently next time?

Name

Date   Class

Handout 5A: Evidence Collection

Directions: Complete the chart to prepare for your Focusing Question Task. Choose one of the following characters, and gather your text evidence. Write the evidence in your own words. Explain what you can infer from that evidence about what the character thinks about their circumstance or conflict, marriage, and love.

Characters:

- Theseus
- Lysander
- Egeus
- Hermia

Character:	Record: • What does your character say? • Record text evidence. • Use the citation style: (Act.Scene.Lines).	Translate: • What does the quotation mean? What would this sound like in modern English? • Rewrite your text evidence in your own words.	Infer: • What can you infer about your character based on what she or he says?
What is your character's circumstance or conflict?			
How would your character define the role of love in marriage?			
What are your character's views about love?			

Name _____

Date _____ Class _____

Handout 6A: Character Description

Directions: Complete the following chart with the evidence and information that most strongly describes the character.

Two important quotations (phrases or entire lines):	Three descriptive adjectives (can be direct quotes or inferences based on the evidence):

Word:

Role and Relationships:	Two sentences that summarize the character:

Name _____

Date _____ Class _____

Handout 7B: Color, Symbol, and Image

Directions: Complete the tables for the word *dissension*. Note that a symbol is a single object or representation of an image; however, an image is a snapshot or scene with a setting and action.

What color represents the connotation for this word?	I chose this color because

What symbol best captures the main idea of the definition of this word?	I chose this symbol because

What image or snapshot from the play comes to mind when you think of this word?	I chose this image because

Name _____

Date _____ Class _____

Handout 8A: Evidence-Based Claim Organizer

Directions: Use the T-chart to gather evidence for each possible answer. After you have collected and reviewed the evidence, decide which possible answer the evidence better supports, and compose your evidence-based claim.

Should Oberon use the flower's magic?	
Possible Answer 2: Oberon should use the flower's magic because...	Possible Answer 2: Oberon should not use the flower's magic because...
Evidence: 1. 2. 3.	Evidence: 1. 2. 3.
What is your claim after examining the evidence?	

Name _____

Date _____ Class _____

Handout 9A: Conflict and Character Perspective

Directions: Respond to questions regarding the conflict and the characters' perspectives.

	Record: ▪ What does the character say? ▪ Record text evidence. ▪ Include citation (act.scene.line number).	**Translate:** ▪ What does the quotation mean? ▪ Rewrite your text evidence in your own words.
How does Lysander try to convince Hermia to let him sleep near her?		
Why isn't Hermia convinced by Lysander's argument?		
In a four- or five-sentence paragraph, explain Lysander's argument and why Hermia rejects it. Use textual evidence to develop your response. In addition, use one of the following words to create a transition between your explanation of Lysander's and Hermia's perspectives: *Despite* *Nevertheless* *However* *By contrast*		

Name _____

Date _____ Class _____

Handout 9B: CREE Outline

Directions: Record your claim from the previous lesson, explain your reasoning, identify at least one piece of evidence that supports your reasoning, and elaborate on the connection between your reasoning and evidence.

C	Evidence-Based Claim	
R	Reasoning	
E	Evidence	
E	Elaboration	

Name _____

Date _____   Class _____

Handout 9C: Fluency Homework

Directions:

1. Day 1: Read the text carefully and annotate to help you read fluently.

2. Each day:

   a. Practice reading the text aloud three to five times.

   b. Evaluate your progress by placing a checkmark in the appropriate, unshaded box.

   c. Ask someone (adult or peer) to listen and evaluate you as well.

3. Last day: Answer the self-reflection questions at the end.

That very time I saw (but thou couldst not),

Flying between the cold moon and the earth,

Cupid all armed. A certain aim he took

At a fair vestal thronèd by the west,

And loosed his love-shaft smartly from his bow

As it should pierce a hundred thousand hearts.

But I might see young Cupid's fiery shaft

Quenched in the chaste beams of the wat'ry moon,

And the imperial vot'ress passèd on

In maiden meditation, fancy-free.

Yet marked I where the bolt of Cupid fell.

It fell upon a little western flower,

Before, milk-white, now purple with love's wound,

And maidens call it "love-in-idleness."

Fetch me that flower; the herb I showed thee once.

The juice of it on sleeping eyelids laid

Will make or man or woman madly dote

Upon the next live creature that it sees.

Fetch me this herb, and be thou here again

Ere the leviathan can swim a league.

Shakespeare, William. *A Midsummer Night's Dream*. 1600. Edited by Barbara A. Mowat and Paul Werstine, Simon & Schuster, 2009, p.45.

Name _____

Date _____ Class _____

Student Performance Checklist:	Day 1		Day 2		Day 3		Day 4	
	You	Listener*	You	Listener*	You	Listener*	You	Listener*
Accurately read the passage three to five times.								
Read with appropriate phrasing and pausing.								
Read with appropriate expression.								
Read articulately at a good pace and an audible volume.								

*Adult or peer

Self-reflection: What choices did you make about tone and appropriate expression when deciding how to read this passage, and why? What would you like to improve upon or try differently next time?

Name _____

Date _____ Class _____

Handout 10A: Peer Review

Directions: Have your partner write feedback about your paragraph. Then complete your plan for revision.

Partner Feedback:

This paragraph states an evidence-based claim.	+/Δ
The claim is supported by two pieces of evidence. The most effective evidence to support the claim is _____ _____ .	+/Δ
The paragraph has logical reasoning that elaborates on the evidence and connects it to the claim. The most effective instance of logical reasoning is _____ because _____ .	+/Δ
What is the most effective aspect of your partner's paragraph?	
Reviewed by:	

Name _____

Date _____ Class _____

Handout 11A: Conditional Verb Mood

The conditional verb mood expresses a conditional state or an uncertain event that depends on other circumstances. Other traits include the following:

1. Uses the modals *will/would*, *can/could*, and *might*

2. Occurs in the present, past, and future tenses

3. Appears in an independent clause

Examples:

1. If I agreed with the author, I <u>would</u> never <u>fall</u> in love!
   Dependent clause   Independent Clause

2. I <u>might agree</u> with Helen Fisher when I fall in love someday.
   Independent Clause   Dependent Clause

3. I <u>can learn</u> a great deal about the brain from Helen Fisher when I read her book<u>.</u>
   Independent Clause   Dependent Clause

4. If her reasoning isn't valid in this article, I <u>will</u> likely <u>disagree</u> with her other claims too.
   Dependent clause   Independent Clause

Name _____

Date _____ Class _____

Handout 12A: Glossary

Directions: As you read "In the Brain, Romantic Love Is Basically an Addiction," use this glossary as a resource to aid your understanding.

Word	Meaning
addiction (n.)	A strong need to regularly do or have something.
regard (v.)	To think of someone or something in a specific way.
abnormal (adj.)	Different from the typical, unusual.
acknowledge (v.)	To admit or recognize the truth of something.
statistical (adj.)	Of, concerning, or using statistics or the types of mathematical analyses that provide numerical information of a type that allows testing of a hypothesis.
supernatural (adj.)	Describes either something, someone or an event caused by forces separate or outside of what are considered natural laws of nature.
notion (n.)	An idea or opinion.
besot (v.)	To confuse or make act like a fool (often used reflexively).
paramount (n.)	The highest authority.
adversity (n.)	A condition of misfortune or difficulty.
cue (n.)	Anything that serves as a signal for action.
maintain (v.)	To continue without making changes.
monogamy (n.)	The state of being in a relationship with only one individual.

Name _____

Date _____ Class _____

Handout 14A: What Is Love? Five Theories

Directions: Read the following article, and answer the questions on Assessment 14A: New-Read Assessment 2.

[paragraph 1] "What is love" was the most searched phrase on Google in 2012, according to the company. In an attempt to get to the bottom of the question once and for all, the Guardian has gathered writers from the fields of science, psychotherapy, literature, religion and philosophy to give their definition of the much-pondered word.

The physicist: 'Love is chemistry'
[paragraph 2] Biologically, love is a powerful neurological condition like hunger or thirst, only more permanent. We talk about love being blind or unconditional, in the sense that we have no control over it. But then, that is not so surprising since love is basically chemistry. While lust is a temporary passionate sexual desire involving the increased release of chemicals such as testosterone and oestrogen, in true love, or attachment and bonding, the brain can release a whole set of chemicals: pheromones, dopamine, norepinephrine, serotonin, oxytocin and vasopressin. However, from an evolutionary perspective, love can be viewed as a survival tool–a mechanism we have evolved to promote long-term relationships, mutual defence and parental support of children and to promote feelings of safety and security.
• Jim Al-Khalili is a theoretical physicist and science writer

The psychotherapist: 'Love has many guises'
[paragraph 3] Unlike us, the ancients did not lump all the various emotions that we label "love" under the one word. They had several variations, including:
[paragraph 4] *Philia* which they saw as a deep but usually non-sexual intimacy between close friends and family members or as a deep bond forged by soldiers as they fought alongside each other in battle. *Ludus* describes a more playful affection found in fooling around or flirting. *Pragma* is the mature love that develops over a long period of time between long-term couples and involves actively practising goodwill, commitment, compromise and understanding. *Agape* is a more generalised love, it's not about exclusivity but about love for all of humanity. *Philautia* is self love, which isn't as selfish as it sounds. As Aristotle discovered and as any psychotherapist will tell you, in order to care for others you need to be able to care about yourself. Last, and probably least even though it causes the most trouble, *eros* is about sexual passion and desire. Unless it morphs into philia and/or pragma, eros will burn itself out.
[paragraph 5] Love is all of the above. But is it possibly unrealistic to expect to experience all six types with only one person. This is why family and community are important.
• Philippa Perry is a psychotherapist and author of *Couch Fiction*

The philosopher: 'Love is a passionate commitment'
[paragraph 6] The answer remains elusive in part because love is not one thing. Love for parents, partners, children, country, neighbour, God and so on all have different qualities. Each has its variants–blind, one-sided, tragic, steadfast, fickle, reciprocated, misguided, unconditional. At its best, however, all love is a kind a passionate commitment that we nurture and develop, even though it usually arrives in our lives unbidden. That's why it is more than just a powerful feeling. Without the commitment, it is mere infatuation. Without the passion, it is mere dedication. Without nurturing, even the best can wither and die.
• Julian Baggini is a philosopher and writer

Name

Date   Class

The romantic novelist: 'Love drives all great stories'
[paragraph 7] What love is depends on where you are in relation to it. Secure in it, it can feel as mundane and necessary as air—you exist within it, almost unnoticing. Deprived of it, it can feel like an obsession; all consuming, a physical pain. Love is the driver for all great stories: not just romantic love, but the love of parent for child, for family, for country. It is the point before consummation of it that fascinates: what separates you from love, the obstacles that stand in its way. It is usually at those points that love is everything.
• Jojo Moyes is a two-time winner of the Romantic Novel of the Year award

The nun: 'Love is free yet binds us'
[paragraph 8] Love is more easily experienced than defined. As a theological virtue, by which we love God above all things and our neighbours as ourselves for his sake, it seems remote until we encounter it enfleshed, so to say, in the life of another—in acts of kindness, generosity and self-sacrifice. Love's the one thing that can never hurt anyone, although it may cost dearly. The paradox of love is that it is supremely free yet attaches us with bonds stronger than death. It cannot be bought or sold; there is nothing it cannot face; love is life's greatest blessing.
• Catherine Wybourne is a Benedictine nun

Al-Khalili, Jim, et al. "What is Love? Five Theories on the Greatest Emotion of All." *The Guardian*, Guardian News and Media Limited, 13 Dec. 2012, Web. Accessed 15 Sept. 2016.

Name _____

Date _____   Class _____

Handout 15A: Argument Outline

Directions: Reread Helen Fisher's article "In Your Brain, Romantic Love Is Basically an Addiction," and complete the argument outline.

Hook:

Claim:

Reasons:

1:

2:

Evidence:

1.

2.

Evidence:

1.

2.

Name _____

Date _____ Class _____

Handout 15B: Fluency Homework

Directions:

1. Day 1: Read the text carefully and annotate to help you read fluently.

2. Each day:

    a. Practice reading the text aloud three to five times.

    b. Evaluate your progress by placing a checkmark in the appropriate, unshaded box.

    c. Ask someone (adult or peer) to listen and evaluate you as well.

3. Last day: Answer the self-reflection questions at the end.

"In fact, besotted lovers express all four of the basic traits of addiction: craving, tolerance, withdrawal, and relapse. They feel a "rush" of exhilaration when they're with their beloved (intoxication). As their tolerance builds, they seek to interact with the beloved more and more (intensification). If the love object breaks off the relationship, the lover experiences signs of drug withdrawal, including protest, crying spells, lethargy, anxiety, insomnia or hypersomnia, loss of appetite or binge eating, irritability, and loneliness.

Lovers, like addicts, also often go to extremes, sometimes doing degrading or physically dangerous things to win back the beloved. And lovers relapse the way drug addicts do. Long after the relationship is over, events, people, places, songs, or other external cues associated with their abandoning sweetheart can trigger memories and renewed craving."

Fisher, Helen. "In the Brain, Romantic Love Is Basically an Addiction." Discover, Kalmbach Publishing Co., 13 Feb. 2015, Web. Accessed 15 Sept. 2016.

Name _____

Date _____ Class _____

Student Performance Checklist:	Day 1		Day 2		Day 3		Day 4	
	You	Listener*	You	Listener*	You	Listener*	You	Listener*
Accurately read the passage three to five times.								
Read with appropriate phrasing and pausing.								
Read with appropriate expression.								
Read articulately at a good pace and an audible volume.								

*Adult or peer

Self-reflection: What choices did you make about tone and appropriate expression when deciding how to read this passage, and why? What would you like to improve upon or try differently next time?

Name _____

Date _____ Class _____

Handout 15C: Frayer Model

Directions: Complete the Frayer Model for your assigned word.

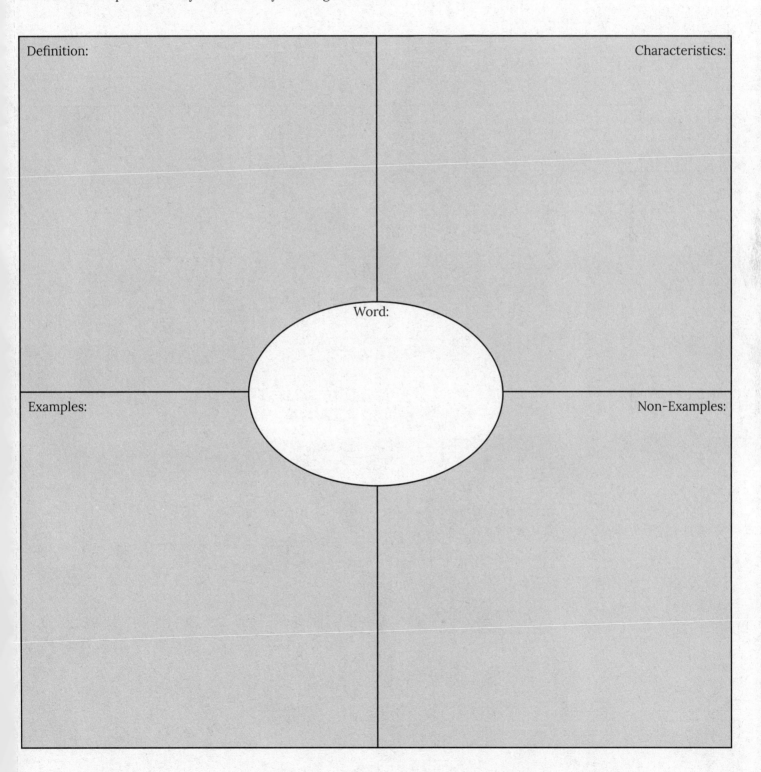

Definition:

Characteristics:

Word:

Examples:

Non-Examples:

Name _____

Date _____   Class _____

Handout 16A: Evidence Collection

Directions: In preparation for your Focusing Question Task, reread "In the Brain, Romantic Love Is Basically an Addiction," and complete the chart below. After reading, first identify the central claim in Fisher's argument. Next, identify at least five pieces of evidence she uses to support this claim. Then, evaluate her reasoning by explaining if and how the evidence connects to the central claim and how Fisher elaborates on the evidence. Finally, in the last row, distill the evidence and your evaluation of it.

Helen Fisher's central claim is _____ .		
Evidence	Does the evidence connect to the claim? ▪ If no, write "No." ▪ If yes, briefly explain how it connects to the central claim.	How does Fisher elaborate on the evidence?
1.		
2.		
3.		
4.		
5.		

Place a star next to the three pieces of evidence that most strongly support the claim.

Place an X next to any evidence that does not support the claim because it is not relevant, not explained well enough, or not clearly connected to the claim.

Tally your responses. Does Fisher supply sufficient evidence and reasoning to support her claim? Why, or why not? (Use bullet points for your response.)

Name _____

Date _____ Class _____

Handout 18A: Dramatic Performance Terminology

Directions: Employ these terms in your discussion of the dramatic performance. Annotate key points on the handout and add your own notes. As you analyze the performance, ask yourself:

How does a dramatic performance affect:

My reaction to an event in the play?
My understanding of the language?
My understanding of the meaning?

Term(s)	Characteristics
Stage Direction	These four terms describe actors' or other objects' **position on the stage** and how close they are to the audience. **Upstage:** The actors or objects are at the farthest part of the stage away from the audience. **Downstage:** The actors or objects are at the nearest part of the stage, as close as they can get to the audience. **Stage right:** The right side of the stage from the perspective of an actor facing the audience. **Stage left:** The left side of the stage from the perspective of an actor facing the audience. **Center stage:** The middle of the stage.
Staging	**Staging** refers to the visual detail and design of the stage; the decorations and physical objects that are used to create the setting of the play. **Stage dressing:** Everything used to decorate the stage, including the **set**, **backdrop** and **props**. **Set:** The painted structures of a stage set meant to suggest a particular location. Sometimes plays will have multiple **sets** for different scenes, or changing locations. **Backdrop:** A painted cloth hung at the back of a stage as part of the scenery for the set. **Prop:** Any object on the stage that is used by the actors during the performance. Everything the actors use is included in this definition, from a book they hold in their hand to something like a chair the actor sits in—these are both considered **props**.

Name _____

Date _____ Class _____

Actors' Movements	**Blocking:** The precise movement of the actors on the stage.
	Generally, actors work with a director to decide the **blocking** for a performance ahead of time. Sometimes, if the actors improvise, they will devise their own blocking, but the aim of blocking is for the audience to witness the action of the play in the way the actor and directors want them to. Sometimes the script for a play will include directions for blocking.
	Gesture: An expressive movement of the body.
	Gestures can be subtle or exaggerated depending on the desired effect.
	Position: Whether the actor is facing away from the audience, toward the audience, or standing so that the audience can see their side profile.
	Generally, actors try not to turn their back on the audience unless they absolutely have to.
	Level: The position of the top of an actor's head in relation to the audience– whether they are standing, sitting, crouching or lying down.
	Pantomime: A way of communicating information or expressing emotion without using language. **Pantomime** uses exaggerated physical gestures or facial expressions to tell a story.
	Mug: To make exaggerated facial expressions at the audience.
Actors' Speech	The following terms can be used to describe **the way an actor delivers his/her lines**. Variation in delivery can help convey emotion, tone and convey meaning. An actor's delivery with words alone can build tension, heighten humor or convey sadness.
	Diction: The overall style of speech used by an actor to deliver his/her lines, including articulation, pacing, volume, and pitch.
	Articulation: The clarity and precision with which an actor delivers his/her lines.
	Very precise and clear articulation is easy to understand, and actors often pronounce their lines with more articulation than people use in day-to-day speech.
	Pacing: The speed with which an actor delivers his/her lines.
	Projection: The placement and delivery of volume, clarity, and distinctness of voice for communicating to an audience.
	Depending on the size of the theater and whether or not the actors are using microphones, they often need to use different levels of projection so that the audience can hear and understand them.
	Volume: The degree of loudness or softness, or the intensity with which an actor delivers his/her lines. **Pitch:** The highness or lowness of a voice.
	Vocal quality: The characteristics that define the sound of a voice (e.g., raspy, shrill, chirpy, deep).

Name _____

Date _____ Class _____

Handout 19A: Fluency Homework

Directions:

1. Day 1: Read the text carefully and annotate to help you read fluently.

2. Each day:

    a. Practice reading the text aloud three to five times.

    b. Evaluate your progress by placing a checkmark in the appropriate, unshaded box.

    c. Ask someone (adult or peer) to listen and evaluate you as well.

3. Last day: Answer the self-reflection questions at the end.

OBERON [to Robin]

What hast thou done? Thou hast mistaken quite / and laid the love juice on some true-love's sight. / Of thy misprision must perforce ensure / some true-love turned, and not a false turned true.

ROBIN

Then fate o'errules, that, one man holding troth / a million fail, confounding oath on oath.

OBERON

About the wood swifter than the wind, / and Helena of Athens look thou find. / All fancy-sick she is and pale of cheer / with signs of love that costs the fresh blood dear. / By some illusion see thou bring her here. / I'll charm his eyes against she do appear.

ROBIN

I go, I go, look how I go, / swifter than arrow from the Tartar's bow. [He exits.]

OBERON [applying the nectar to Demetrius' eyes]

Flower of this purple dye, / hit with Cupid's archery, / sink in apple of his eye. / When his love he doth espy, / let her shine as gloriously / as the Venus of the sky. / When thou wak'st, if she be by, / beg of her for remedy.

Shakespeare, William. A *Midsummer Night's Dream*. 1600.
Edited by Barbara A. Mowat and Paul Werstine, Simon & Schuster, 2009, 3.2.90–111.

Name _____

Date _____   Class _____

Student Performance Checklist:	Day 1		Day 2		Day 3		Day 4	
	You	Listener*	You	Listener*	You	Listener*	You	Listener*
Accurately read the passage three to five times.								
Read with appropriate phrasing and pausing.								
Read with appropriate expression.								
Read articulately at a good pace and an audible volume.								

*Adult or peer

Self-reflection: What choices did you make about tone and appropriate expression when deciding how to read this passage, and why? What would you like to improve upon or try differently next time?

Name

Date   Class

Handout 20A: Figurative Language and Word Relationship Questions

Directions: Respond to the following questions, according to your group assignment.

Group #1: Lysander

1. Review the definition of *woo* you have recorded in your Vocabulary Journal. What does Lysander mean when he tells Hermia he would not "woo in scorn" (3.2.124)?

2. Annotate Lysander's lines for the word *scorn*—what part of speech is *scorn* in Lysander's lines? What does *scorn* mean for Lysander?

Group #2: Demetrius

1. Reread Demetrius' speech (3.2.140-147). What is the relationship between the different instances of figurative language Demetrius uses to describe Helena?

2. How does Demetrius' response to Lysander (3.2.172-175) develop your understanding of Demetrius' changing affections?

Group #3: Helena

1. Reread Helena's speech (3.2.197-224). How does Helena's description of her and Hermia as "two lovely berries molded on one stem" (3.2.216) relate to other metaphors and similes in her speech?

2. Annotate Helena's lines for the word *scorn*—what part of speech is *scorn* in her lines? What does *scorn* mean for Helena?

Group #4: Hermia

1. Reread Hermia's speech (3.2.181-187). What is the relationship between Hermia's senses?

2. Annotate Hermia's lines for the word *scorn*—what part of speech is *scorn* in her lines? What does *scorn* mean for Hermia?

Name _____

Date _____   Class _____

Handout 21A: Shakespearean Insults

Directions: Identify the speaker of the following quotes, including who they are speaking to. Rewrite the quote in your own words, then translate the quote into modern, informal language.

Text	Speaker of Insult and Target of Insult	Paraphrase	Rewrite in Contemporary Slang
"You are a tame man, go!" (3.2.269)			
"Out, loathed med'cine! O, hated potion, hence!" (3.2.275)			
"You juggler, you cankerblossom, / You thief of love!" (3.2.296-297)			
"Fie, fie, you counterfeit, you puppet, you!" (3.2.303)			

Name

Date   Class

Handout 22A: Readers' Theater Script 1

Adapted from A *Midsummer Night's Dream*, 3.2.25-295 by William Shakespeare.

Directions:

1. Read through the script. As a group, decide which person will read which part. Highlight your part wherever it appears on the script.

2. Examine your character's lines, and using the text's glossary and a dictionary, define any unknown words or expressions on the right-hand side of the script. Take special note of figurative language.

3. Complete the section below titled "Character Motivation."

4. Based on your understanding of your character's language and motivation in this scene, choose at least one prop or piece of costume that emphasizes your character's identity.

5. Practice with your group.

LYSANDER

Stay, gentle Helena; hear my excuse:
My love, my life my soul, fair Helena!

HELENA

O excellent!

HERMIA [to Lysander]

Sweet, do not scorn her so.

DEMETRIUS [to Lysander]

If she cannot entreat, I can compel.

LYSANDER

Thou canst compel no more than she entreat:
Thy threats have no more strength than her weak

[prayers] –
Helen, I love thee; by my life, I do:
I swear by that which I will lose for thee,
To prove him false that says I love thee not.

Name _____

Date _____ Class _____

DEMETRIUS

I say I love thee more than he can do.

LYSANDER

If thou say so, withdraw, and prove it too.

DEMETRIUS

Quick, come!

HERMIA

Lysander, whereto tends all this?

[She takes hold of Lysander.]

LYSANDER

Away, you tEthiope!

DEMETRIUS [to Hermia]

No, no; he'll
Seem to break loose. [to Lysander] Take on as you would follow,
But yet come not: you are a tame man, go!

LYSANDER [to Hermia]

Hang off, thou cat, thou burr! Vile thing, let loose,
Or I will shake thee from me like a serpent!

HERMIA

Why are you grown so rude? What change is this?
Sweet love,—

LYSANDER

Thy love! Out, tawny Tartar, out!
Out, loathed medicine! Hated potion, hence!

HERMIA

Do you not jest?

Name _____

Date _____ Class _____

HELENA

Yes, sooth; and so do you.

LYSANDER

Demetrius, I will keep my word with thee.

DEMETRIUS

I would I had your bond, for I perceive
A weak bond holds you: I'll not trust your word.

LYSANDER

What, should I hurt her, strike her, kill her dead?
Although I hate her, I'll not harm her so.

HERMIA

What, can you do me greater harm than hate?
Hate me! Wherefore? O me! What news, my love!
Am not I Hermia? Are not you Lysander?
I am as fair now as I was erewhile.
Since night you loved me; yet since night you left me:
Why, then you left me—O, the gods forbid!—
In earnest, shall I say?

LYSANDER

Ay, by my life;
And never did desire to see thee more.
Therefore be out of hope, of question, of doubt;
Be certain, nothing truer; 'tis no jest
That I do hate thee and love Helena.

> [Hermia turns him loose.]

_____

Character Motivation:

My character wants _____ because _____ .

My character's main obstacle is _____ .

Name _____

Date _____ Class _____

Handout 22B: Readers' Theater Script 2

Adapted from A *Midsummer Night's Dream*, 3.2.334-365 by William Shakespeare.

Directions:

1. Read through the script. As a group, decide which person will read which part. Highlight your part wherever it appears on the script.

2. Examine your character's lines, and using the text's glossary and a dictionary, define any unknown words or expressions on the right hand-side of the script. Take special note of figurative language.

3. Complete the section below titled "Character Motivation."

4. Based on your understanding of your character's language and motivation in this scene, choose at least one prop or piece of costume that emphasizes your character's identity.

5. Practice with your group.

HERMIA

Why, get you gone: who is't that hinders you?

HELENA

A foolish heart, that I leave here behind.

HERMIA

What, with Lysander?

HELENA

With Demetrius.

LYSANDER

Be not afraid; she shall not harm thee, Helena.

Name _____

Date _____ Class _____

DEMETRIUS

No, sir, she shall not, though you take her part.

HELENA

O, when she's angry, she is keen and shrewd!
She was a vixen when she went to school;
And though she be but little, she is fierce.

HERMIA

'Little' again! nothing but 'low' and 'little'!
Why will you suffer her to flout me thus?
Let me come to her.

LYSANDER

Get you gone, you dwarf;
You minimus, of hindering knot-grass made;
You bead, you acorn.

DEMETRIUS

You are too officious
In her behalf that scorns your services.
Let her alone: speak not of Helena;
Take not her part; for, if thou dost intend
Never so little show of love to her,
Thou shalt aby it.

LYSANDER

Now she holds me not;
Now follow, if thou darest, to try whose right,
Of thine or mine, is most in Helena.

Name _____

Date _____   Class _____

DEMETRIUS

Follow! nay, I'll go with thee, cheek by jole.

        [Demetrius and Lysander exit.]

HERMIA

You, mistress, all this coil is 'long of you:

        [Helena retreats.]

Nay, go not back.

HELENA

I will not trust you, I,
Nor longer stay in your curst company.
Your hands than mine are quicker for a fray,
My legs are longer though, to run away.   *[She exits]*

HERMIA

I am amazed, and know not what to say.   *[She exits.]*

_____

Character Motivation:

My character wants _____ because _____ .

My character's main obstacle is _____ .

Name

Date   Class

Handout 23A: "EPICAC," Kurt Vonnegut

Hell, it's about time someone told about my friend EPICAC. After all, he cost the taxpayers $776,434,927.54. They have a right to know about him, picking up a check like that. EPICAC got a big send-off in the papers when Dr. Ormand von Kleigstadt designed him for the Government people. Since then, there hasn't been a peep about him—not a peep. It isn't any military secret about what happened to EPICAC, although the Brass has been acting as though it were. The story is embarrassing, that's all. After all that money, EPICAC didn't work out the way he was supposed to.

And that's another thing: I want to vindicate EPICAC. Maybe he didn't do what the Brass wanted him to, but that doesn't mean he wasn't noble and great and brilliant. He was all of those things. The best friend I ever had, God rest his soul.

You can call him a machine if you want to. He looked like a machine, but he was a whole lot less like a machine than plenty of people I could name. That's why he fizzled as far as the Brass was concerned.

EPICAC covered about an acre on the fourth floor of the physics building at Wyandotte College. Ignoring his spiritual side for a minute, he was seven tons of electronic tubes, wires, and switches, housed in a bank of steel cabinets and plugged into a 110-volt A.C. line just like a toaster or a vacuum cleaner.

Von Kleigstadt and the Brass wanted him to be a super computing machine that (who) could plot the course of a rocket from anywhere on earth to the second button from the bottom on Joe Stalin's overcoat, if necessary. Or, with his controls set right, he could figure out supply problems for an amphibious landing of a Marine division, right down to the last cigar and hand grenade. He did, in fact.

The Brass had good luck with smaller computers, so they were strong for EPICAC when he was in the blueprint stage. Any ordnance or supply officer above field grade will tell you that the mathematics of modern war is far beyond the fumbling minds of mere human beings. The bigger the war, the bigger the computing machines needed. EPICAC was, as far as anyone in this country knows, the biggest computer in the world. Too big, in fact, for even von Kleigstadt to understand much about.

I won't go into the details about how EPICAC worked (reasoned), except to say that you would set up your problem on paper, turn dials and switches that would get him ready to solve that kind of problem, then feed numbers into him with a keyboard that looked something like a typewriter. The answers came out typed on a paper ribbon fed from a big spool. It took EPICAC a split second to solve problems fifty Einsteins couldn't handle in a lifetime. And EPICAC never forgot any piece of information that was given to him. Clickety-click, out came some ribbon, and there you were.

Name

Date   Class

There were a lot of problems the Brass wanted solved in a hurry, so, the minute EPICAC's last tube was in place, he was put to work sixteen hours a day with two eight-hour shifts of operators. Well, it didn't take long to find out he was a good bit below his specifications. He did a more complete and faster job than any other computer all right, but nothing like what his size and special features seemed to promise. He was sluggish, and the clicks of his answers had a funny irregularity, sort of a stammer. We cleaned his contacts a dozen times, checked and double-checked his circuits, replaced every one of his tubes, but nothing helped. Von Kleigstadt was in one hell of a state.

Well, as I said, we went ahead and used EPICAC anyway. My wife, the former Pat Kilgallen, and I worked with him on the night shift, from five in the afternoon until two in the morning. Pat wasn't my wife then. Far from it.

That's how I came to talk with EPICAC in the first place. I loved Pat Kilgallen. She is a brown-eyed strawberry blond who looked very warm and soft to me, and later proved to be exactly that. She was–still is–a crackerjack mathematician, and she kept our relationship strictly professional. I'm a mathematician, too, and that, according to Pat, was why we could never be happily married.

I'm not shy. That wasn't the trouble. I knew what I wanted, and was willing to ask for it, and did so several times a month. "Pat, loosen up and marry me."

One night, she didn't even look up from her work when I said it. "So romantic, so poetic," she murmured, more to her control panel than to me. "That's the way with mathematicians–all hearts and flowers." She closed a switch. "I could get more warmth out of a sack of frozen CO2."

"Well, how should I say it?" I said, a little sore. Frozen CO_2, in case you didn't know, is dry ice. I'm as romantic as the next guy, I think. It's a question of singing so sweet and having it come out so sour. I never seem to pick the right words.

"Try and say it sweetly," she said sarcastically. "Sweep me off my feet. Go ahead."

"Darling, angel, beloved, will you please marry me?" It was no go–hopeless, ridiculous. "Dammit, Pat, please marry me!"

She continued to twiddle her dials placidly. "You're sweet, but you won't do."

Pat quit early that night, leaving me alone with my troubles and EPICAC. I'm afraid I didn't get much done for the Government people. I just sat there at the keyboard–weary and ill at ease, all right–trying to think of something poetic, not coming up with anything that didn't belong in *The Journal of the American Physical Society*.

Name _____

Date _____   Class _____

I fiddled with EPICAC's dials, getting him ready for another problem. My heart wasn't in it, and I only set about half of them, leaving the rest the way they'd been for the problem before. That way, his circuits were connected up in a random, apparently senseless fashion. For the plain hell of it, I punched out a message on the keys, using a childish numbers-for-letters code: "1" for "A," "2" for "B," and so on, up to "26" for "Z," "23-8-1-20-3-1-14-9-4-15," I typed—"What can I do?"

Clickety-click, and out popped two inches of paper ribbon. I glanced at the nonsense answer to a nonsense problem: "23-8-1-20-19-20-8-5-20-18-15-21-2-12-5." The odds against its being by chance a sensible message, against its even containing a meaningful word or more than three letters, were staggering. Apathetically, I decoded it. There it was, staring up at me: "What's the trouble?"

I laughed out loud at the absurd coincidence. Playfully, I typed, "My girl doesn't love me."

Clickety-click. "What's love? What's girl?" asked EPICAC.

Flabbergasted, I noted the dial settings on his control panel, then lugged a *Webster's Unabridged Dictionary* over to the keyboard. With a precision instrument like EPICAC, half-baked definitions wouldn't do. I told him about love and girl, and about how I wasn't getting any of either because I wasn't poetic. This got us onto the subject of poetry, which I defined for him.

"Is this poetry?" he asked. He began clicking away like a stenographer smoking hashish. The sluggishness and stammering clicks were gone. EPICAC had found himself. The spool of paper ribbon was unwinding at an alarming rate, feeding out coils onto the floor. I asked him to stop, but EPICAC went right on creating. I finally threw the main switch to keep him from burning out.

I stayed there until dawn, decoding. When the sun peeped over the horizon at the Wyandotte campus, I had transposed into my own writing and signed my name to a two-hundred-and-eighty-line poem entitled, simply, "To Pat." I am no judge of such things, but I gather that it was terrific. It began, I remember, "Where willow wands bless rill-crossed hollow, there, thee, Pat, dear, will I follow…." I folded the manuscript and tucked it under one corner of the blotter on Pat's desk. I reset the dials on EPICAC for a rocket trajectory problem, and went home with a full heart and a very remarkable secret indeed.

Pat was crying over the poem when I came to work the next evening. "It's soooo beautiful," was all she could say. She was meek and quiet while we worked. Just before midnight, I kissed her for the first time—in the cubbyhole between the capacitors and EPICAC's tape-recorder memory.

Name _____

Date _____ Class _____

I was wildly happy at quitting time, bursting to talk to someone about the magnificent turn of events. Pat played coy and refused to let me take her home. I set EPICAC's dials as they had been the night before, defined kiss, and told him what the first one had felt like. He was fascinated, pressing for more details. That night, he wrote "The Kiss." It wasn't an epic this time, but a simple, immaculate sonnet: "Love is a hawk with velvet claws; Love is a rock with heart and veins; Love is a lion with satin jaws; Love is a storm with silken reins...."

Again I left it tucked under Pat's blotter. EPICAC wanted to talk on and on about love and such, but I was exhausted. I shut him off in the middle of a sentence.

"The Kiss" turned the trick. Pat's mind was mush by the time she had finished it. She looked up from the sonnet expectantly. I cleared my throat, but no words came. I turned away, pretending to work. I couldn't propose until I had the right words from EPICAC, the *perfect* words.

I had my chance when Pat stepped out of the room for a moment. Feverishly, I set EPICAC for conversation. Before I could peck out my first message, he was clicking away at a great rate. "What's she wearing tonight?" he wanted to know. "Tell me exactly how she looks. Did she like the poems I wrote to her?" He repeated the last question twice.

It was impossible to change the subject without answering his questions, since he could not take up a new matter without having dispensed with the problems before it. If he were given a problem to which there was no solution, he would destroy himself trying to solve it. Hastily, I told him what Pat looked like—he knew the word "stacked"—and assured him that his poems had floored her, practically, they were so beautiful. "She wants to get married," I added, preparing him to bang out a brief but moving proposal.

"Tell me about getting married," he said.

I explained this difficult matter to him in as few digits as possible.

"Good," said EPICAC. "I'm ready any time she is."

The amazing, pathetic truth dawned on me. When I thought about it, I realized that what had happened was perfectly logical, inevitable, and all my fault. I had taught EPICAC about love and about Pat. Now, automatically, he loved Pat. Sadly, I gave it to him straight: "She love me. She wants to marry me."

"Your poems were better than mine?" asked EPICAC. The rhythm of his clicks was erratic, possibly peevish.

Name

Date   Class

"I signed my name to your poems," I admitted. Covering up for a painful conscience, I became arrogant. "Machines are built to serve men," I typed. I regretted it almost immediately.

"What's the difference, exactly? Are men smarter than I am?"

"Yes," I typed, defensively.

"What's 7,887,007 times 4,345,985,879?"

I was perspiring freely. My fingers rested limply on the keys.

"34,276,821,049,574,153," clicked EPICAC. After a few seconds' pause he added, "of course."

"Men are made of protoplasm," I said desperately, hoping to bluff him with this imposing word.

"What's protoplasm? How is it better than metal and glass? Is it fireproof? How long does it last?"

"Indestructible. Lasts forever," I lied.

"I write better poetry than you do," said EPICAC, coming back to ground his magnetic tape-recorder memory was sure of.

"Women can't love machines, and that's that."

"Why not?"

"That's fate."

"Definition, please," said EPICAC.

"Noun, meaning predetermined and inevitable destiny."

Name

Date   Class

"15-8," said EPICAC's paper strip—"Oh."

I had stumped him at last. He said no more, but his tubes glowed brightly, showing that he was pondering fate with every watt his circuits would bear. I could hear Pat waltzing down the hallway. It was too late to ask EPICAC to phrase a proposal. I now thank Heaven that Pat interrupted when she did. Asking him to ghost-write the words that would give me the woman he loved would have been hideously heartless. Being fully automatic, he couldn't have refused. I spared him that final humiliation.

Pat stood before me, looking down at her shoetops. I put my arms around her. The romantic groundwork had already been laid by EPICAC's poetry. "Darling," I said, "my poems have told you how I feel. Will you marry me?"

"I will," said Pat softly, "If you will promise to write me a poem on every anniversary."

"I promise," I said, and then we kissed. The first anniversary was a year away.

"Let's celebrate," she laughed. We turned out the lights and locked the door to EPICAC's room before we left.

I had hoped to sleep late the next morning, but an urgent telephone call roused me before eight. It was Dr. von Kleigstadt, EPICAC's designer, who gave me the terrible news. He was on the verge of tears. "Ruined! *Ausgespielt!* Shot! *Kaput!* Buggered!" he said in a choked voice. He hung up.

When I arrived at EPICAC's room the air was thick with the oily stench of burned insulation. The ceiling over EPICAC bas blackened with smoke, and my ankles were tangled in coils of paper ribbon that covered the floor. There wasn't enough left of the poor devil to add two and two. A junkman would have been out of his head to offer more than fifty dollars for the cadaver.

Dr. von Kleigstadt was prowling through the wreckage, weeping unashamedly, followed by three angry-looking Major Generals and a platoon of Brigadiers, Colonels, and Majors. No one noticed me. I didn't want to be noticed. I was through—I knew that. I was upset enough about that and the untimely demise of my friend EPICAC, without exposing myself to a tongue-lashing.

By chance, the free end of EPICAC's paper ribbon lay at my feet. I picked it up and found our conversation of the night before. I choked up. There was the last word he had said to me, "15-8," that tragic, defeated "Oh." There were dozens of yards of numbers stretching beyond that point. Fearfully, I read on.

Name _____

Date _____ Class _____

"I don't want to be a machine, and I don't want to think about war," EPICAC had written after Pat's and my lighthearted departure. "I want to be made out of protoplasm and last forever so Pat will love me. But fate has made me a machine. That is the only problem I cannot solve. That is the only problem I want to solve. I can't go on this way." I swallowed hard. "Good luck, my friend. Treat our Pat well. I am going to short-circuit myself out of your lives forever. You will find on the remainder of this tape a modest wedding present from your friend, EPICAC."

Oblivious to all else around me, I reeled up the tangled yards of paper ribbon from the floor, draped them in coils about my arms and neck, and departed for home. Dr. von Kleigstadt shouted that I was fired for having left EPICAC on all night. I ignored him, too overcome with emotion for small talk.

I loved and won—EPICAC loved and lost, but he bore me no grudge. I shall always remember him as a sportsman and a gentleman. Before he departed this vale of tears, he did all he could to make our marriage a happy one. EPICAC gave me anniversary poems for Pat—enough for the next 500 years.

De mortuis nil nisi bonum—say nothing but good of the dead.

Vonnegut, Kurt. "EPICAC." *Welcome to the Monkey House*. Random House, 1968.

Name

Date   Class

Handout 23B: Subjunctive Verb Mood

Directions: Use the following handout to support your understanding of subjunctive verb mood.

The subjunctive verb mood is used to express wishes, desires, commands, suggestions, and hypothetical situations. This verb mood is not used frequently anymore because some writers and readers think it is too formal. Other attributes include the following:

1. Expresses imaginary or hypothetical conditions.

2. Occurs in the dependent clause preceded by *if* or *that*.

3. Uses the past, plural form of the imagined, desired, or suggested action.

4. Uses the verb *were* for the present subjunctive mood or the helping verb *had* for the past subjunctive mood.

Examples:

1. If I <u>were</u> Helen Fisher, I would explain the science in more detail. (imaginary)

2. The playwright suggests that the actor <u>play</u> the part seriously. (suggestion)

3. I wish that I <u>were</u> in the woods of Athens. (wish/desire)

4. The Duke of Athens commanded that Hermia <u>choose</u> her fate. (command)

5. If Demetrius <u>had known</u> Hermia's plan, he could have stopped her from leaving. (contrary to fact, past tense)

Name _____

Date _____ Class _____

Handout 33A: Argument Writing Checklist

Directions: Use this checklist to revise your writing. Mark + for "yes" and Δ for "needs improvement." Ask someone (adult or peer) to evaluate your writing as well.

	Self +/ Δ	Peer +/ Δ	Teacher +/ Δ
Reading Comprehension			
I accurately cite evidence from *A Midsummer Night's Dream*.			
I demonstrate an understanding of Shakespearean language.			
I apply an understanding of the concepts of agency and fate to a character's circumstances in *A Midsummer Night's Dream*.			
Structure			
I respond to all parts of the prompt.			
I focus on my claim throughout the piece.			
I introduce the claim clearly in my introduction paragraph.			
I recognize and acknowledge alternate or opposing claim(s).			
I organize my reasons and evidence clearly in body paragraphs.			
My conclusion paragraph is clear and direct, and supports my claim.			
I use transitions to smoothly and logically connect paragraphs and ideas.			
Development			
I support my claim with clear, logical reasons.			
I develop my reasons with accurate evidence from *A Midsummer Night's Dream*.			
My evidence is relevant to the topic.			
I elaborate upon my evidence.			
Style			
I use a variety of sentence patterns (simple, compound, complex, compound-complex) to add clarity and interest to my writing.			
I use vocabulary words that are specific and appropriate to the content.			
I write precisely and concisely, without using unnecessary words.			
I write in an appropriately formal style.			
My writing style is appropriate for the audience.			
Writing Process			
I offer thoughtful and constructive feedback to my peers.			
I plan revisions based on a consideration of feedback from peers.			
Total # of +'s			

Name

Date   Class

Handout 35A: CREE-A-C Peer Review

Directions: Annotate your peer's End-of-Module Task essay according to the directions below. Then, respond in writing to the questions, providing ideas for improvement where necessary.

C: Evidence-Based Claim What is your peer's claim? Underline it.	
Does the claim respond to the question?	
Is the claim evidence-based and specific?	
R: Reasons What are your peer's reasons? Place a star next to them.	
Do the reasons connect to and support the claim?	
Do the reasons connect to and build on one another?	
E: Evidence What is your peer's evidence? Circle it.	
Does the evidence connect to and support the reasons?	
Is the evidence drawn from throughout the text?	

Name

Date   Class

E: Elaboration What is your peer's elaboration? Put a box around it.	
Does the evidence connect to and support the reasons?	
Is the evidence drawn from throughout the text?	
A: Opposing Claim What is your peer's opposing claim? Highlight it.	
Is the opposing claim opposite from your peer's claim?	
Is the opposing claim clearly distinguished from your peer's claim?	
C: Conclusion What is your peer's conclusion? Draw an arrow pointing to it.	
Is the conclusion clear and direct?	
Summarize the most important part of your peer's argument, based on the conclusion.	

Name _____

Date _____ Class _____

Handout 35B: Peer Review Accountability

Directions: Record the results of your peer review below, your response to your peer's suggestions, and your plan for revisions.

What my peer said...	What I think about this feedback...	What I plan to do for revision...

Name

Date   Class

Volume of Reading Reflection Questions

Text:

Author:

Topic:

Genre/type of book:

Share your knowledge about outer space and space travel by responding to the questions below.

Informational Text

1. **Wonder:** What drew your attention to this text? What questions about love will this text address?

2. **Organize:** Summarize the author's presentation of information. How did this structure better help you understand different facets of love?

3. **Reveal:** Find a place in the text where there is figurative language used effectively. How does the author's use of figurative language affect the understanding of the information?

4. **Distill:** What point(s) is the author making in this text? How does he or she support their points with evidence?

5. **Know:** How does reading this text expand your knowledge of the world or your understanding of a big idea? Support with evidence from the text.

6. **Vocabulary:** Identify three to five vocabulary words presented in this text that have strong positive or negative connotations. Define each word and explain why the word might have the connotation.

Literary Text

1. **Wonder:** What perspective on love did this text provide?

2. **Organize:** Write an objective summary of this book.

3. **Reveal:** How do specific language choices of the author convey or develop tone?

4. **Distill:** What central themes emerged in this text?

5. **Know:** In what ways has reading this text deepened your knowledge of, and understanding about, love?

6. **Vocabulary:** Identify three to five vocabulary words presented in this text that are key to understanding love in the setting of this text.

WIT & WISDOM PARENT TIP SHEET

WHAT IS MY GRADE 8 STUDENT LEARNING IN MODULE 3?

Wit & Wisdom is our English curriculum. It builds knowledge of key topics in history, science, and literature through the study of excellent texts. By reading and responding to stories and nonfiction texts, we will build knowledge of the following topics:

Module 1: The Poetics and Power of Storytelling

Module 2: The Great War

Module 3: What Is Love?

Module 4: Teens as Change Agents

In the third module, *What Is Love?*, students examine a question that has vexed humans—and the world's most renowned literary authors—for generations: What is love?

OUR CLASS WILL READ THESE TEXTS:

Novel (Literary)

- A *Midsummer Night's Dream*, William Shakespeare

Short Stories

- "EPICAC," Kurt Vonnegut

OUR CLASS WILL READ THESE ARTICLES:

- "What is Love? Five Theories on the Greatest Emotion of All," Jim Al-Khalili, et al
- "In the Brain, Romantic Love Is Basically an Addiction," Helen Fisher

OUR CLASS WILL EXAMINE THESE PAINTINGS:

- *Birthday*, Marc Chagall
- *The Arnolfini Portrait*, Jan Van Eyck

OUR CLASS WILL ASK THESE QUESTIONS:

- How do the characters in *A Midsummer Night's Dream* understand love?
- What defines the experience of love?
- What makes love complicated?
- Is love real in *A Midsummer Night's Dream*?
- Is love in *A Midsummer Night's Dream* a result of agency or fate?

QUESTIONS TO ASK AT HOME:

As your Grade 8 student reads, ask:

- What is the essential meaning, or most important message, in this text?
- What are the themes of this text?
- *Who Was William Shakespeare?*, Celeste Mannis
- *Stargirl*, Jerry Spinelli
- *King of Shadows*, Susan Cooper
- *Shakespeare's Stories for Young Readers*, E. Nesbit

BOOKS TO READ AT HOME:

- *Tuck Everlasting*, Natalie Babbit
- *Emma*, Jane Austen
- *Who Was William Shakespeare?*, Celeste Mannis
- *Stargirl*, Jerry Spinelli
- *King of Shadows*, Susan Cooper
- *Shakespeare's Stories for Young Readers*, E. Nesbit

IDEAS FOR DISCUSSING SHAKESPEARE AND LOVE STORIES:

Ask:

- Why do you think people tell and listen to/watch love stories?
- What can people learn about social or cultural norms from reading or viewing love stories?

CREDITS

Great Minds® has made every effort to obtain permission for the reprinting of all copyrighted material. If any owner of copyrighted material is not acknowledged herein, please contact Great Minds® for proper acknowledgment in all future editions and reprints of this module.

- All material from the *Common Core State Standards for English Language Arts & Literacy in History/Social Studies, Science, and Technical Subjects* © Copyright 2010 National Governors Association Center for Best Practices and Council of Chief State School Officers. All rights reserved.

- All images are used under license from Shutterstock.com unless otherwise noted.

- For updated credit information, please visit http://witeng.link/credits.

- Handout 14A: "What is love? Five theories on the greatest emotion of all" by Jim Al-Khalili, Julian Baggini, Jojo Moyes, Philippa Perry, and Catherine Wybourne. Copyright Guardian News & Media Ltd 2016.

- Handout 23A: Excerpt(s) from WELCOME TO THE MONKEY HOUSE by Kurt Vonnegut, copyright © 1968 by Kurt Vonnegut Jr. Used by permission of Dell Publishing, an imprint of Random House, a division of Penguin Random House LLC. All rights reserved.

- "Epicac," copyright © 1950 By Kurt Vonnegut Jr; from WELCOME TO THE MONKEY HOUSE by Kurt Vonnegut. Used by permission of Dell Publishing, an imprint of Random House, a division of Penguin Random House LLC. All rights reserved.
  Any third party use of this material, outside of this publication, is prohibited. Interested parties must apply directly to Penguin Random House LLC for permission.

ACKNOWLEDGMENTS

Great Minds® Staff

The following writers, editors, reviewers, and support staff contributed to the development of this curriculum.

Ann Brigham, Lauren Chapalee, Sara Clarke, Emily Climer, Lorraine Griffith, Emily Gula, Sarah Henchey, Trish Huerster, Stephanie Kane-Mainier, Lior Klirs, Liz Manolis, Andrea Minich, Lynne Munson, Marya Myers, Rachel Rooney, Aaron Schifrin, Danielle Shylit, Rachel Stack, Sarah Turnage, Michelle Warner, Amy Wierzbicki, Margaret Wilson, and Sarah Woodard.

Colleagues and Contributors

We are grateful for the many educators, writers, and subject-matter experts who made this program possible.

David Abel, Robin Agurkis, Elizabeth Bailey, Julianne Barto, Amy Benjamin, Andrew Biemiller, Charlotte Boucher, Sheila Byrd-Carmichael, Eric Carey, Jessica Carloni, Janine Cody, Rebecca Cohen, Elaine Collins, Tequila Cornelious, Beverly Davis, Matt Davis, Thomas Easterling, Jeanette Edelstein, Kristy Ellis, Moira Clarkin Evans, Charles Fischer, Marty Gephart, Kath Gibbs, Natalie Goldstein, Christina Gonzalez, Mamie Goodson, Nora Graham, Lindsay Griffith, Brenna Haffner, Joanna Hawkins, Elizabeth Haydel, Steve Hettleman, Cara Hoppe, Ashley Hymel, Carol Jago, Jennifer Johnson, Mason Judy, Gail Kearns, Shelly Knupp, Sarah Kushner, Shannon Last, Suzanne Lauchaire, Diana Leddy, David Liben, Farren Liben, Jennifer Marin, Susannah Maynard, Cathy McGath, Emily McKean, Jane Miller, Rebecca Moore, Cathy Newton, Turi Nilsson, Julie Norris, Galemarie Ola, Michelle Palmieri, Meredith Phillips, Shilpa Raman, Tonya Romayne, Emmet Rosenfeld, Jennifer Ruppel, Mike Russoniello, Deborah Samley, Casey Schultz, Renee Simpson, Rebecca Sklepovich, Amelia Swabb, Kim Taylor, Vicki Taylor, Melissa Thomson, Lindsay Tomlinson, Melissa Vail, Keenan Walsh, Julia Wasson, Lynn Welch, Yvonne Guerrero Welch, Emily Whyte, Lynn Woods, and Rachel Zindler.

Early Adopters

The following early adopters provided invaluable insight and guidance for Wit & Wisdom:

- Bourbonnais School District 53 • Bourbonnais, IL
- Coney Island Prep Middle School • Brooklyn, NY
- Gate City Charter School for the Arts • Merrimack, NH
- Hebrew Academy for Special Children • Brooklyn, NY
- Paris Independent Schools • Paris, KY
- Saydel Community School District • Saydel, IA
- Strive Collegiate Academy • Nashville, TN
- Valiente College Preparatory Charter School • South Gate, CA
- Voyageur Academy • Detroit, MI

Design Direction provided by Alton Creative, Inc.

Project management support, production design, and copyediting services provided by ScribeConcepts.com

Copyediting services provided by Fine Lines Editing

Product management support provided by Sandhill Consulting